Mommy and Me Don't Match

K MONSMA

ISBN 978-1-64003-631-4 (Paperback)
ISBN 978-1-64003-632-1 (Digital)

Covenant Books, Inc.
11661 Hwy 707
Murrells Inlet, SC 29576
www.covenantbooks.com

To my three beautiful children. May you always celebrate each other's differences and never forget that your hearts will always beat the same.

My mom has light skin. And I have brown skin. She has brown hair and green eyes. I have black hair and brown eyes.

I lifted my hand to my mom's and said "Mommy, how come we don't match?" Mommy took my hand in hers and smiled.

4

"You are right, honey. Your skin is darker than mine. Your brown eyes don't match my green eyes. And your curly black hair is different than my wavy brown hair."

"But I have a question for you! I have two hands. How many do you have?"
"One... Two! I have two hands too, Mommy!"

"I have two legs. Do you have two legs too?"

"Yes, Mommy! I do!" I said.

"Hmm… Let's find
some more. How many
toes do you have?"
I counted all the way to ten!
"Ten! I have ten toes!"
"Me too!" said Mommy.

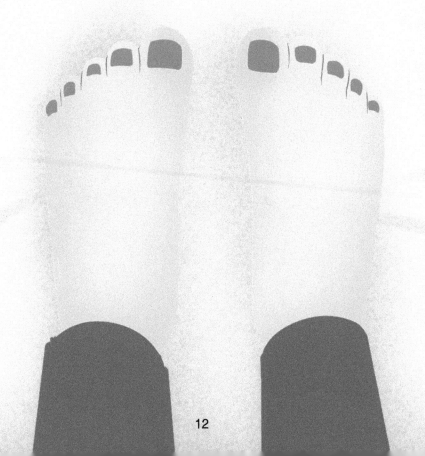

"I have one tummy,
and on that tummy is
one belly button."
Mommy lifted my shirt to
show me that I too had
one tummy and one belly
button just like hers.

My mom pulled me in real close. She took my hand and placed it on her chest. "Do you feel that? That's my heart beating inside me." Then she placed my hand on my chest. "Mom! My heart is beating inside me just like yours!"

"That's right, honey. Even though we look different on the outside, our hearts beat the same. I love your hands, your legs, and toes. I love your brown skin, your dark curly hair, and your beautiful brown eyes. But most of all I love your heart. Your heart that matches mine."

"I love you, Mommy."
"I love you the most," she said.

Thank you for reading my book! I never imagined that these words from my heart would be printed for others to read! I hope this book was something special that your family could connect with. My hope is that any child who looks different than their parents, for any reason, will get a glimpse into our hearts and know just how loved they are.

K Monsma

About the Author

K Monsma is a wife and mother to three children ages four, three, and one. She and her husband adopted their youngest daughter who is biracial. After realizing that it was difficult to find children's picture books that featured multi-racial families like hers, K Monsma decided to take a chance at publishing a book. A book that will hopefully touch the hearts of many families just like hers.

9 781640 036314